Finding Your Way When Your Spouse Dies

Edited by Linus Mundy

Abbey Press
St. Meinrad, IN 47577

Text © 2004 Abbey Press
Published by One Caring Place
Abbey Press
St. Meinrad, Indiana 47577

ISBN 0-87029-381-8

Printed in the United States of America

Introduction

∽

We have published over the years hundreds of "CareNotes" booklets on many topics, some very specific and some quite general. The common themes are: illness, distress, grief, suffering. But one theme—the death of a spouse—is consistently most in "demand."

Losing one's partner, one's soul mate, one's spouse, "demands," after all, the greatest inner strength one can apply. And it requires the help and wisdom of fellow grief-travelers such as you will find in the five sections of this booklet.

"I knew my life would never be the same again," wrote a friend and co-worker to me after the death of her spouse. "But I didn't know that it could somehow, someway, still be OK." May this booklet be a helpful guide on your way back, somehow, to OK-ness.

—Linus Mundy, Editor

Contents

∾

CHAPTER I

Finding Your Way After the Death of a Spouse

∾

By Erin Diehl

"Erin—help me, help me—I think I'm dying," Dave cried out. And then he was gone. It had been only three months since we had received the diagnosis of cancer of the lungs in an advanced state. We were both stunned because Dave had always been unusually healthy. The doctors had found nothing wrong in previous checkups.

Before we received the result of the X rays, I promised Dave, my husband of 43 years, that I would be strong no matter what. And strong I was through the grueling three months of illness, during the funeral Mass, at the burial, at the reception so kindly arranged by women from my parish. I went on and on and on being strong!

Eighteen months later I have encountered what one writer calls "delayed grief." And I have learned a very valuable lesson: We must allow ourselves to grieve, and we all grieve in different ways, for various lengths of time.

Working your way through | In one of the books I read on grief, I came across the phrase "creative survivor." What a hopeful term! That is what Dave would want me to be. I can almost hear him saying in his calm and loving and practical way, "O.K., Erin, now get on with your life. Just put one foot in front of the other and keep going."

This does not mean that I do not have excruciating times of missing him. It just means I profit by the wisdom I know he would impart to me and which I hope to impart to you in this chapter.

✎ *Take steps to relieve loneliness.* Loneliness is a constant companion. I rationalize that everyone is lonely at times, even married people. Yet coming home to find no one to share news with is a debilitating "downer." Evenings and nights have been the worst times for me.

Occupying those long evening hours can

ease the void. Always having been a "book-in-hand meditator," I turned to books on grief very naturally. I spent many sleepless nights poring over them and found much solace. I also used tapes on grief.

Praying always helps me, and keeping a journal can provide a healing catharsis as well. Television can be diverting at times, but since it is such a passive occupation, it might prove depressing. I find that radio, especially National Public Radio, provides a welcome relief. Music of all types can be a real mood-elevator.

Pets, too, can be a source of comfort. My dogs run over and paw me for attention at my first sign of tears. Who could resist such unabashed affection?

❧ *Let others help you.* Reach out to others and allow them to help carry that heavy pain which is constantly with you in the early days of grief. Stoicism will not help, but there are many persons who will if you give them an idea

It helps to consider that our loved ones are happy—free of pain and hassles—and that we will be together again. Also, if you died, would you want your loved ones to deeply mourn the rest of their lives? You would want them to enjoy life as much as possible. They want this for you now.

—Father Ken Czillinger
"After the First Year... Thoughts for the Bereaved"

of your needs and desires. The outpouring of love you receive from family and friends can be a tremendous source of comfort and unity. When invitations come from friends and relatives, you may find them difficult to accept, however. I find it best to accept as many as possible. Realize that the telephone is a two-way instrument, and that you may call people as well as expecting them to call you.

Some people will not know what to say to you. They may even avoid you entirely. This is just a fact and you should not allow it to hurt you too deeply. Expect changes in your relationships. Your social life may not be couple-oriented to any great extent anymore. Although your married friends want to include you, their life-style is different. You can make valuable new friendships with other widowed or single persons.

I cannot say enough good things about support groups. I belong to two different parish-based groups. I also made a Beginning Experience weekend (for widowed or divorced people) and a weekend retreat on "Coping With Grief." Shared tears and laughter are healing; trying to help others is a potent pain reliever.

❧ *Ease your adjustment as best you can.* At this time of change, you would be wise not to

4

make hasty decisions about anything—selling your home, dispensing with personal effects, making major purchases, or any other significant changes.

> *"I knew my life would never be the same again. But I didn't know that it could somehow, someway, still be OK."*
> —Mary Wiker, *Letters*

Avail yourself of practical helps to ease your adjustment. Our lawyer helped me through the legal mishmash after Dave's death. Family friends and business associates also provided valuable advice.

Because this period of grief and adjustment can be so stressful, you will need to maintain your strength with a nutritious diet. And physical exercise, especially walking, helps to clear out the cobwebs. Grieving is very fatiguing, so rest at night even if you cannot sleep. Relaxation techniques might be helpful. Let yourself cry when you need to. Allow yourself to be reflective, and don't worry if you do not seem to be getting much accomplished for a while.

As you make adjustments in your life, you may find you are developing greater independence. I have gained new confidence in my own actions and decisions, and I like the feeling of overcoming natural fears which might keep me from doing things. I feel pride and pleasure about the new paths I am following in my education and my work.

❧ *Rely on your faith.* Whatever your religion, it can be your main strength in living on. When Dave died, his brother Tom, who is a priest, and our four grown children came immediately. Tom said Mass while I sat by the bed holding Dave's hand, with the children gathered around. Suddenly, the sun rose outside the window in a blaze of red and gold. What a beautiful resurrection! God had painted a picture I'm sure Dave appreciated as he joined his heavenly Father—a Father he had known so well that as a child he had called him "Skipper."

Walking with God through my grief has deepened my faith. I never felt really angry with God because I knew that my loving God did

But if grief is resolved, why do we still feel a sense of loss come anniversaries and holidays, and even when we least expect it? Why do we feel a lump in the throat, even six years after the loss? It is because healing does not mean forgetting, and because moving on with life does not mean that we don't take a part of our lost loved one with us.
—Adolfo Quezada

not zap me with this circumstance.

God will walk with you, too. Yet you must realize that your grief may not be finished at some certain point you have in mind. At 18 months, I feel the loss with even greater intensity at times. It does not last as long as before, however.

If you are feeling "stuck" in grief, an understanding therapist might be in order—especially if you have more than fleeting thoughts of suicide. Mainly, I think it helps to consider that you are an integral part of God's plan and precious to God beyond measure.

∾ *Do not dwell on regrets.* The doctors had told me privately that Dave could live as long as six months or as little as three. But he was determined to adopt a positive attitude in hopes of getting well. In reply to telephone calls from friends, I often heard him say, "Oh, I have just a 'touch of cancer'"!

I did not want to tell Dave his cancer was terminal because he obviously did not want to hear it. One night when I asked him why he seemed to be shutting me out, he told me he did not intend to, that he was just too ill to talk about it.

I now feel we missed something by not being able to communicate as well about this as we always had about everything else. But I try not to dwell on what I could have done better. I did the best I could. So did he.

If you feel regretful about something you did or did not do before your spouse died, try to be gentle with yourself. This person who loved you so much would not judge you so harshly; neither should you submit yourself to such painful hindsight.

Take Heart | I have days when it seems that such a big piece has been ripped from my life that only a gaping hole is left. Yet I also have days of celebrating new beginnings. My life and my roles are different now, and many of the changes I have experienced are positive ones. I am learning every day how to be a "creative survivor." And I trust that you will too.

Erin Diehl is a social psychotherapist, a spiritual director, and a freelance writer. She leads a parish support group for widows and widowers.

CHAPTER II

The Questions Widows and Widowers Ask Most

By Rev. Mary Kendrick Moore

While serving as the on-call chaplain in a metropolitan emergency room, I encountered many tragic occasions of meeting a man or woman as they rushed to the hospital, only to learn their spouse had not survived a car crash, or a gunshot wound, or the last stage of their illness.

The end of those evenings was always familiar yet mysterious. I would hand the spouse the remaining personal belongings and exchange parting words of comfort. Then, when I could go no further, I watched as they turned to walk away, beginning a journey all their own—that no one could walk for them.

Like them, as you took those first brave steps away from your spouse after their death, you began a journey of discovering all that it means to live each day without your loved one—a journey of questions that encircle a well of heartache and struggle.

Working your way through | Questions are a normal part of your grief after the death of your spouse. In fact, questions are often the first words with which grief finds expression as one cries, How can this be? Think about when we normally ask questions—when we need information or answers, when we need help, when we are searching for something, or when we are lost. All of these needs are present in grief, and our questions give our needs a voice. Allow your questions to surface, for they will be your guide and your teacher, and be gentle with yourself when answers do not come quickly or do not come at all.

~ *Why?* Although we think of questions as having answers, grief is filled with unanswerable questions like, *Why is this happening to me?* Early after the death of a spouse, difficult questions that begin with *Why* or *What more* may surface: *Why could we not say goodbye? Why did he leave me? What more could the hospital have done? What more could I have said to let her know I loved her?* Questions like these prevail in the emptiness left by the death of your spouse, as you reach within your own depths and cry out to others and to God, asking why you are alone. Attempting to answer the unanswerable can lead you to despair or an unwarranted sense of guilt, arising from your feelings of helplessness.

Rather than calling for a logical answer, these questions signal just how much you loved your spouse and how deeply you will miss them. When you find yourself asking these difficult questions, allow yourself to imagine, "What am I missing about her today?" The tears may flow once again, but your tears are the river that flows toward healing.

The difficult *why* questions are often directed toward God: *God, why is this happening to me? God, why did you*

You will never again be the person you once were. You will have lost, but in addition to the losing—because of the losing—you will have gained. You will be yourself, and you will be more than yourself. Some people describe this process as transformation, others call it resurrection. Whatever words you choose, the result is the same. Something new will have happened. Something original will have come to life. Something unexpected will have been born.

—James E. Miller
Winter Grief,
Summer Grace

leave me alone? In mourning, the Psalmist once cried out to God, "How long will you hide your face from me?" (13:1) In the same way, we are called to bring the deepest part of our pain before God. Whatever your emotions—sadness, anger, guilt—expressing these to God is an important part of your faith journey.

☙ *Will I make it?* Some questions pose very real and threatening challenges for the widowed. Fear and anxiety are often the partners of questions like, *Will I have enough money to pay the bills? Will I be able to make it on my own? Will I be able to take care of the children all by myself?*

These questions add a difficult layer to grief for the recently widowed. Financial challenges, the day-to-day responsibilities of raising children alone, and the demands of settling an estate can feel overwhelming. Alan, who in his early 40's is raising his children alone following his wife's death in a car accident, says, "There is twice as much to do and half as much energy to do it." Set reasonable expectations for yourself and, when possible, accept or even ask for support from friends and family.

☙ *When will the pain end?* Perhaps the only certainty about grief is that it does not go away quickly. You may wonder if life will ever be pleasant and meaningful again. The questions that greet you on these days—*When will I ever be happy again? When will the loneliness ever end?*—give voice to the ongoing and relentless nature of grief.

> *"In the midst of winter I found at last there was within myself an invincible summer."*
> —Albert Camus

When you wonder if you will ever be happy again, let yourself also wonder two other things: *What if I were happy again?* and, *When was I happiest with my spouse?* Give yourself permission to be hopeful about your future, while cherishing the memories that brought you happiness in the past. Just as waves of the ocean swell to their height and then gently recede, with each passing month you will begin to feel the waves of grief begin to recede more quickly.

∾ *Who am I now?* In a relationship that has lasted for years, your identity as a spouse is a significant part of how you see yourself. You may feel lost without your partner, or not know how to act as a single person. You begin to ask how to socialize again, or wonder if you want to date.

After all, days, calendars, meals, outings, and vacations were often planned together, each of you taking the other's needs and desires into consideration. Suddenly, it's just you. The pain and fear of this loneliness can lead some to prematurely enter new relationships, simply because they cannot bear being alone. A huge part of your life is gone. Allow yourself time to heal and accept that life will never be the same again.

With experience comes the gradual trying on of a different life without your spouse. Following the death of my father, my mother found herself struggling with what her life would be without him. Months after his death, she called to let me know she had completed her driver's education course and was purchasing a new car at age 70. She allowed space for something new and different in her life, and found a renewed sense of confidence and independence.

The widowed sometimes experience aspects of themselves they never felt or believed possible during their marriage relationship. This does not diminish the love

Be patient toward all that is unsolved in your heart and try to love the questions themselves like locked rooms or books that are written in a foreign tongue. The point is to live everything. Live the questions now. Perhaps you will then gradually, without noticing it, live your way some distant day into the answers.

—Rainer Maria Rilke

you feel for your spouse but is a tribute to the strength we can find in our own individuality, even during grief.

∾ *What now?* Some questions during grief do have a particular answer you will discover, such as *When should I return to work or start working? Should I move? What should I do with the personal belongings?* These questions, you might think, would be easier if someone could give you the answers. But in truth, the answers are to be discovered by you within your own timing. No two journeys through grief are exactly alike. Take your time. The answers will come.

Just after her children were grown, a woman in midlife faced not only the death of her husband, but also a very complex set of circumstances related to his mental illness and drug addiction. Though she grieved deeply what their lives would never have become together, in time she expanded her career as a nurse and reentered college, eventually moving to a new city and making new friends.

These decisions will be very personal for you as you embrace your life as a single person or consider a new relationship. Resist any temptation to make important decisions too quickly simply to avoid the painful feelings of grief. And find a trusted friend, perhaps someone who has known grief in a way similar to you, and discuss your decisions until you feel assurance about changes that you want to make.

Take Heart A huge canyon is created following a significant loss. Though it will never explain or justify a loss, over time and with healing this same canyon of despair creates room for something new. Whether it be making new friends at a community book club or volunteering at a social agency, gradually your heart will open once again to the activities and relationships that will begin to fill the empty spaces.

The teacher in me has always felt that if you can ask a question, you can learn. In grief—in the emptiness of loss—if you can ask a question and invite others to be a part of the journey, you can heal. The very nature of a question implies that you are seeking something beyond yourself to give meaning to your experience, and someone beyond yourself to offer solace. As long as the questions surface, there are expressions of grief left to honor. Just as one day you will look back and the wound will not feel as deep, similarly your questions will grow less frequent and persistent.

Five years after her husband's death, an 82-year-old friend says, "I have a new life now in my new home and with new friends. I have missed him terribly and have cried buckets full of tears. But one day, I realized I could be happy again." As you live your questions, may you come to believe that you, too, will be happy once again.

*Rev. **Mary Kendrick Moore** is a minister in the United Church of Christ, a healthcare chaplain, and a freelance writer. She can be reached at <u>mmmoore@mindspring.com</u>.*

CHAPTER III

When Your Spouse Dies Suddenly

∾

By Ann Solari-Twadell

It was the first warm, sunny Saturday of spring. I had to work in the morning, and knowing that my husband Steve was going biking with our son, I lingered after work, stopping at the shopping mall. When I got home all the windows were open, inviting the first aromas of spring into the house.

There was a message on the answering machine. I listened to my son's voice saying that he and his father had been biking when his father had developed chest pains. He left the name of the hospital for me to call. When I called, I was told that my son was on the way home to get me. They had done all they could, they said, but my husband had died.

Working your way through | Unlike those who lose their most intimate loved one over time due to a protracted illness, when your spouse dies suddenly, your life changes in the blink of an eye. There is no way to prepare for the changes ahead. But with time you can find your way. Here are a few suggestions that may be of help.

❧ *Accept your vulnerability.* I had abruptly lost the mirror to my soul when Steve died. We shared a very intimate relationship. He could perceive things about me that I myself was not aware of, and vice versa. I had come to rely on his insights. He had been my strongest supporter. When I had doubted myself, he had been there to encourage me to appreciate the gifts I had, and to build on them. With him gone, I felt very vulnerable.

Sometimes I was emotionally vulnerable even though I didn't want to be. This was an important thing for me to accept. There was no way to anticipate all of the times our favorite song would be played in a restaurant, every time someone would be wearing his brand of after-shave. When I least expected it, a song, smell, sound, or place brought waves of sadness and tears. It was difficult to express the sadness, especially when others began to signal that "sufficient" time has passed and that "I shouldn't feel that way anymore." If necessary, I would excuse myself and find a place where I could be how I needed to be at the moment.

❧ *Take care of yourself.* To help find emotional release and physical energy, make some form of exercise a regular part of your schedule. I used what energy I had to engage in aerobic exercise almost daily. That became very important in giving me an emotional lift. Maintaining a discipline to exercise regularly is difficult when you feel a lack of energy and enthusiasm. However, being consistent will result in a positive outcome emotionally. If exercise was not part of your routine before the death of your spouse, getting started will be challenging, but it will also be very rewarding.

Take it one day at a time. Sometimes, you may need to take it one minute at a time. However, I found that no mat-

About three days after Steve died, I awoke and became terrified because suddenly I could not remember his laugh. Was I losing my mind? Fortunately, Steve was on a videotape from our daughter's wedding. I found the tape and listened to him laugh. It brought comfort to me to know that even though my memory was failing me as a result of this sudden loss, there were mementos that would support me during this time.

ter what was going on that brought stress, eventually it would pass. I took it slow, realizing that in meeting grief on a daily basis there is only so much energy to deal with anything else. I only dealt with those issues that absolutely had to be attended to. All other things could wait. At a time like this, the priority has to be your well-being.

ॐ *Begin to let go of the pain.* I had some residual feelings of guilt and anger regarding Steve and myself, which is common when you lose a loved one suddenly. The relationship may feel unfinished and imperfect, and sometimes there is anger because we feel abandoned by our deceased spouse. I found journaling useful in my effort to reflect on the issues.

Over time it was important to forgive myself and Steve for being imperfect, as well as to let go of the potentially crippling feelings of guilt and anger. If these feelings aren't dealt with, they can keep us stuck in negativity. There is no need to force yourself to let go of painful feelings, however; it will happen naturally when you allow yourself the time and space to feel the pain.

ॐ *Seek spiritual support.* After Steve's death, I found it very hard to pray. For one thing, I had trouble concentrating on anything. Fortunately, I belonged to a faith community that had daily services. Each morning I started the day by attending these services. I welcomed the prayers of others for Steve and myself. In my work environment as well as my faith community, there were many who kept us in their prayers. Knowing that so many were supporting me in prayer gave me a lot of strength and hope. I found that even though I could not pray, being with others who could helped me feel that God was walking with me through this time of loss.

> *"I found that even though I could not pray, being with others who could helped me feel that God was walking with me through this time of loss."*

If prayer is difficult right now, try being with others who are praying. Attend religious services frequently. This can help bring you into a community of faith. In being in their midst, you will find yourself supported by their energy and faithfulness. If you have not been a regular member of a worship community, this can be an opportunity to seek one out.

Establish a daily quiet time for yourself. This

Financially, I was fortunate because I had paid the bills and managed the finances before Steve's death. I didn't have to suffer from financial insecurity. For those who have not planned ahead, and do not have a will or a trust set up, financial confusion can be a major issue. If your spouse handled all the financial matters, you may be confused about such things as bill payment, insurance policies, debts, and inheritance, among others.

Given this, panic can easily be added to the long list of feelings you are struggling with. Find a professional financial advisor whom you can trust at this time of vulnerability. Insist on working through everything together so you learn as you go along. Expect to feel overwhelmed by your grief at times as you sort through it all. Take your time. Put off major financial decisions for at least six months—a year if possible.

is your time—a time for reflection, a time to catch up with your own feelings. For me, it was most helpful to journal thoughts, feelings, dreams, and worries. It was helpful to get them on paper where they could more clearly be acknowledged. You may find this helpful, or you may prefer to just sit quietly, perhaps with a candle and soft music.

❧ *Find a way to enjoy life and be grateful again.* One morning about five months after Steve died, I realized that there wasn't much fun and laughter in my life anymore. When Steve was with me, there was fun. I didn't have to create it or look for it. This gave me another issue to address. How do I build fun back into my life? Again, having good friends to share this insight with was most helpful. Slowly, over the next months, having fun and learning to laugh again became more natural.

I worked very hard at being grateful. Rather than focus on the vacuum that had been created, I tried to focus on all the wonderful things Steve and I had done; on our wonderful children; on the fact that he didn't suffer and that he was with his beloved son when he died, rather than traveling abroad as he often did. Speaking to others of this gratitude helped me to reinforce this attitude.

Develop a gratitude list. In the midst of the sudden loss of your spouse, there are still things to be grateful for each day. For me, it might be that the sun was shining, or that a family member or friend had called. Sometimes I was grateful for having slept well. Think of a few simple things that you can feel grateful for today. It will help with the healing.

| *Take Heart* | When you lose your spouse suddenly, it tears a gaping hole in your life. There's no other way to describe it. There is no |

quick fix that will fill that hole. But if you are willing to listen to the small, still voice within, and if you can be open to the support of others, over time that gaping hole can be healed. The scar remains, but through the grace of God and the love of family and friends, you will be able to once again live a full and meaningful life.

Ann Solari-Twadell is a nurse and director of the International Parish Nurse Resource Center in Park Ridge, Illinois. She has a daughter and son, both of whom are married. Recently she become a first-time grand-mother to Nathan Joseph Kuhlman and Kaitlyn Lacombe Twadell.

CHAPTER IV

Six Sources of Strength After the Death of Your Spouse

❧

By Jane Genzel

I n the first week, the first month, the first year, my husband's death taught me many lessons. As painful as Don's death was, and still is, I also think of that first year as a mountaintop experience.

Opportunities and experiences came from his death that I otherwise would not have had. I want to share these with you, in this chapter.

Working your way through | When your spouse dies, you wonder how you will go on living. The pain created by their absence is gut-wrenching. You long for one more conversation, one more chance to discuss how to handle each daily problem. Of course, that isn't possible. But the good news is, there is hope, and things can get better. Here are some lessons from my own experience that I hope you will find helpful.

❧ *You learn to face the challenges.* When my husband died, I wasn't bothered by many of the issues that some people might think would be difficult. I wasn't angry about being "abandoned" by a loved one. I knew that it was not Don's choice to leave his two sons and me.

With two children under 10, I didn't have to deal with a silent house. For many widows and widowers, it takes time to get used to an empty bed. But I looked forward to going to bed every night because I was so tired. And when I slept, I didn't feel the pain.

What I found most difficult was that when my husband died, my life changed—permanently. I liked my old life a lot and I wanted it back. I found solace in the company of other widows who understood the depth of my loss. And I found a good counselor whom I saw twice a month. He provided an objective sounding board, something that my husband had been good at, until I found others to fill the void Don left. Other widows have told me that the presence and thoughtfulness of friends and family, people who loved and cared for their deceased spouse, countered their feeling of loss.

∾ *You come to expect the unexpected.* Don's death was an opportunity for me to learn to accept change, to learn to accept whatever God gives me, and to learn to accept situations that I don't control. These are difficult lessons and they continue to challenge me.

Part of the pain from Don's death came from the loss of what I thought my future would be like: the loss of a two-parent family, the loss of my sons' father being present for all those special moments, the loss of our 25th wedding anniversary, the loss of all the things we thought we'd do together.

My life with Don was happy. We planned to love each other "until death do us part." We didn't expect the "death" part to come so soon. My life diverged from a path where I expected certain events to take place, and the new path led to a completely unknown future.

It eventually occurred to me that I might find happiness going down this new

> *There may always be a small place within you that remains hollow. Value it. A quiet, abiding emptiness can be God's way of sustaining your connection to your loved one.*
> —Karen Katafiasz
> *Grief Therapy*

path. The new path was unknown, but it might be OK.

❧ *You find unexpected sources of strength.* In the first week after Don died, I learned that people are generous and kind. Don's death gave friends, relatives, and acquaintances the opportunity to show that they loved Don and cared about his family. For three months, parents from the boys' school brought us dinner. Every Wednesday night, a young woman baby-sat for me at no charge while I attended class to finish my master's degree. People I barely knew came to help put a new roof and siding on my house. People saw a need and used their God-given gifts to ease the pain in my life. The outpouring of help and concern affirmed my belief that people are intrinsically good. Experiencing the love and care from everyone was a mountaintop experience that came out of a tragedy.

I learned that I'm a strong person. The circumstances of my life made me stronger. There were many times that I felt I couldn't handle one more thing. I couldn't learn one more home maintenance skill. Don's death gave me the opportunity to develop the strength and insight to cope with difficult situations. I also learned the phone number of a good plumber.

Don's death gave me the opportunity to appreciate life more fully. My experience with his death showed me that people can leave suddenly, so I try not to take people for granted. I try to accept people as they are, not as I want them to be. Life is too precious to waste time trying to change them.

"Sorrow has taught me to be happy. I know this seems to be a contradiction, but live long enough and you'll discover that life is often its own best oxymoron."

—Ana Veciana-Suarez, widow and reporter

Don's death also gave me the opportunity to improve my coping skills. My life with Don was happy and content. After he died, I was determined to be happy again. I made a concerted effort to fill the void with activities I enjoyed. I spent time with friends, I joined a choir, I soaked in the tub. The boys and I made a poster listing fun things we wanted to do: dance, take a trip, eat pizza. I found happiness by gradually filling my life with activities I enjoyed.

And I learned that I was in charge, so I went out and bought the dishwasher my husband never wanted. I no longer had to consult anyone on any decisions. While this can be a burden, it's also liberating. You can do whatever you want to do.

After a lifetime of marriage and companionship, a husband worried about what would happen to his wife if he died first. When he wasn't feeling well, he would say to her, "What are you going to do without me? How will you get along?" She had some of the same concerns.

After his death, she realized she was more able to care for herself than she expected. It helped that she had lived an independent, single life for several years before getting married. It helped that she had friends to spend time with. It helped that she filled her time by doing volunteer work at a grade school and retirement community. It wasn't always easy, but she figured out how to take care of herself.

❧ *You live with painful emotions.* My heart broke when my six year old said, "I just want to talk to my Dad one more time." And I certainly understood how he felt. I just wanted Don's arms around me, making me feel safe, loved, accepted, valuable.

There are still painful moments. When my sons see a father treating his children poorly, they don't understand why God took a good dad away from them. No matter how well you learn to cope, there are some things that just hurt. Although my sons had their father for a short time, there are children who do not have any positive experiences with their fathers. My sons can be grateful for the good example that Don set for them and for the fun times we had with him.

❧ *You can let faith ease the pain.* Don's death strengthened my faith. When I felt like I couldn't handle one more thing, I knew that God cared about me, and God's care sustained me. I found comfort in the scripture readings I heard and in the music I sang. Every time I was struggling with something, I would go to church, hear God's word, and gain insight into my latest difficult situation.

I cannot count the number of revelations I experienced, developing a peaceful understanding of a situation. That habit of finding peace and understanding in God's word has continued over the years.

❧ *You never forget, but you do move on.* I eventually realized that having someone's arms around me was not the only thing I wanted. I also wanted my children to be happy; I wanted them to do well in school; I wanted them to have friends and have a "normal" life. I wanted to finish my master's degree; I wanted to travel; I wanted a new job; I wanted to lose ten pounds. I refocused.

People leave us gifts as they pass through our lives. I still carry in my planner a Christmas card from Don. In the card, he told me how much he appreciated everything I did and that he enjoyed being married to me. Don may be dead, but he is forever in my mind and heart telling me I'm wonderful. I am so grateful for having spent time with him. I learned that when you love someone, they become a part of you; they are always with you, even after they die.

My husband's death brought incredible pain into my life. In the long run, it also led to new joy. Because of Don's death, I connected with people that I normally wouldn't have. It brought new experiences into my life. It made me a new person. It brought me closer to God.

Take Heart | Sometimes the pain is so intense it's hard to see anything good coming from your spouse's death. But with time, prayer, courage, and caring people in your life, I believe you will find, as I did, that you can look beyond the loss and see the light.

Jane Genzel is remarried and works as a director of Habitat for Humanity, building houses in Peoria, Illinois.

CHAPTER V

Overcoming Loneliness After Loss

By Erin Diehl

Eight years ago, when my husband, Dave, died with cancer after only three months' illness, I was so overwhelmed with loneliness I thought the huge chasm of pain would never be filled. The days were an endless maze of meaningless routine, and my emotions ran amok like a malfunctioning roller coaster.

The nights were even worse. I couldn't sleep and spent the lonely hours trying to read and pray, or wandering from room to room seeking I knew not what. I was alone and my big, old Victorian house was filled with memories and heartbreaking reminders of our 43 happy years together. How would I ever make it alone?

Working your way through | Now I look back, and although I still miss my husband's goodness and loving presence, I feel only a gentle ache in my heart. Today I can agree with an anonymous quote I put on my refrigerator door eight years ago: "It's not so bad—and you're not the only one!" How did I get to this point of having a peaceful heart?

Having decided eight years ago to be a "creative survivor," as outlined in one of the many books I read on grief during those sleepless nights, I tried to do all the practical things I could. I did not feel like myself for a very long time, but some of things I found helpful may help you, too.

❧ *Reach out to friends.* Having many friends has always been one of my most cherished blessings. Perhaps this is a result of my having been an only child and learning early to reach out to others. After my husband's death, I had to learn that when my loneliness seemed overwhelming I could not sit around and wait for someone to call me. I needed to initiate the encounter.

There were times when I was disappointed. I was sometimes surprised when certain people I thought would be attentive just weren't there for me. Others, from whom I didn't expect as much, came through with much loving support. The same holds for family members. Some will probably support you in tremendous ways. Others may not be available in the way that you wish. Don't let it get you down. If you seek support, you will find it.

One friend of mine, Elaine, has been a constant source of strength to me. We live in the same small town but had known one another only casually before Elaine's husband died three years ago. Her courage and faith appealed to me greatly as I saw her trying to cope with the loneliness of widowhood. Elaine and I have become fast friends. Perhaps there is someone who has been through a loss comparable to yours, with whom you can now establish bonds of friendship and support.

∾ *Commemorate your loss.* If you are grieving the death of a loved one, find a way to express the loss you feel, and also to symbolize the ongoing presence of that loved one in your life. Friends who lost their 30-year-old son to AIDS held a beautiful ceremony in

> *"Our loss can become our gain—a blessing that's born in pain."* But if the while I think on thee, dear friend, All losses are restored and sorrows end.*
>
> —William Shakespeare

our church basement after the funeral. It was a joyful commemoration of their son Joe's life, complete with cherished reminders of his life—his old football jersey, awards for various achievements, and photos from different times in his life. The wonderful photo of Joe that hangs in their living room, alongside the photos of their other children, seems to say, "Yes, we miss Joe, but he is still with us."

Find a way to celebrate the gift that your loved one has been to you. Perhaps you could plant a tree or write a poem. However you choose to memorialize your loved one, draw comfort from the fact that nothing can take your cherished memories from you or erase the untold ways your loved one has touched your life and remains very much with you.

ᔟ *Trust that the pain will pass.* My friend Mary was in a lot of pain after her husband abruptly left her with six children to raise. Even though the marriage had not been an ideal one, Mary felt the agony of loneliness. But her faith carried her through the most difficult times, and she is a wiser and stronger person today.

"We can pass through pain because it will not last forever," she says. Mary believes that all of life involves gift and loss. "It is a circle that continues—new joys and new sorrows come into our lives." If your pain feels overwhelming, take some comfort in knowing it will not always feel as intense as it does today.

Meanwhile, give yourself time to grieve and to heal. There is no set timetable and no need to surround yourself with "busyness" all the time. Being alone for a while may allow you to learn valuable things about yourself that will help with future relationships.

There is a peace that prevails over pain.

✎ *Cultivate an appreciation for solitude.* A young friend of mine, Stephen, suffered from a string of broken relationships. Finally he came to a realization: "There is a difference between loneliness and solitude," he says. "You have to develop a sense that you are O.K. with yourself. The thing I've learned is that I can be comfortable when I am by myself."

Find activities you can do alone that bring you satisfaction and peace of mind and heart. Perhaps gardening will bring you comfort, or painting, music, reading, walking—the list is limited only by your imagination. At your time of deepest loss, try to find something special to do that brings you joy. You can never replace the person you have lost, but you can find comfort in solitude if you learn to befriend it. A quiet time for prayer can encourage a greater appreciation for the joys of time alone.

❧ *Get the support you need.* After an experience of great loss, it is natural to feel a variety of emotions. If you would like some ongoing help exploring and working through some of the difficult emotions that may surface, consider getting some private counseling, attending a support group that addresses your needs, or both.

I once had the opportunity to sit in on a support group for unemployed persons. Many of the members recently had been laid off because of corporate downsizing. What a blow to a person's self-esteem! Yet some members were able to find new jobs through contacts made in the group, while others started new careers that brought more satisfaction than their previous work. Most helpful for members was learning that they were not "the only one." You'll learn this, too, if you are able to connect with others who

Let nothing disturb you,
Let nothing frighten you.
All things are passing,
God never changes.
Patience gains all things.
Who has God wants nothing.
God alone is sufficient.
—St. Teresa of Avila

have experienced a loss similar to your own.

෴ *Turn to God for strength.* My faith in God was and is the best coping tool I have. Prayer and meditation can be excellent paths to inner peace and balance. If you are feeling too distressed to pray or sit quietly, don't forget that there are a host of excellent spiritual books and tapes.

Julia Cameron, in *The Artist's Way,* recommends writing three pages a day in a diary. You can use this time to carry on a conversation with God or simply to let out some of the feelings that may be welling up inside. There is great value in "externalizing" your pain, getting it out in the open, on a page, in a drawing—whatever mode of expression best suits you. Consider each and every one of these efforts to be a prayer. They are.

For some years I have belonged to a prayer group that meets every week. We are a close-knit group of 12 caring friends who meet to share and pray at a deep level. We pray for the needs of others and for our own needs. "Ask and you shall receive," Jesus said. Be aware that the Spirit dwells within you and that you can call on the many gifts of the Spirit for comfort and strength in your time of pain and loss.

Brother David Steindl-Rast, a Benedictine monk, emphasizes the value of a grateful heart. It is hard to be thankful and sad at the same time. Spend a little time pondering the many things in your life for which you are grateful. With time, you may even feel gratitude for the admittedly painful lessons you are learning as you move through your present loss.

Each year I make a retreat at the Abbey of Gethsemani in Trappist, Kentucky. In the beautiful surroundings and solitude I am able to pray, as the late Thomas Merton did, that even though I have no idea where I am going, I can trust God and have no fear. God is ever with me and will not leave me to face my perils alone.

Take Heart

Feisty Teresa of Avila gave me the quote I live by, and which my husband had engraved on a bracelet for me: "All things pass." And indeed they do—including the overwhelming pain that you may be feeling right now. It is only human to cry out for relief. Surely it will be forthcoming from the God who loved us first.

Erin Diehl *is a social psychotherapist, a spiritual director, and a freelance writer. She leads a parish support group for widows and widowers.*